FOREWORD

SHELLEY CRAIG, PHD, LCSW

"YOU HAVE THE AMAZING OPPORTUNITY TO SUPPORT AND ADVOCATE FOR SOMEONE WHO NEEDS YOU, WHETHER A FAMILY MEMBER, NEIGHBOR OR FRIEND."

If only families, friends and colleagues truly understood the process when a loved one comes out, we could save years of pain and regret. Marc Adams has written in intuitive form, what those of us in the social sciences are beginning to understand.

Reactions matter.

Recent research has found that the impact of disclosure reactions, or the initial response of the recipient to the coming out message, has a significant impact on youth *(Rosario, Schrimshaw, Hunter, 2009)*. In particular, rejecting reactions are associated with subsequent alcohol, cigarette and marijuana use.

Furthermore, the number and quality of such interactions over time can also provide an understanding of future success. This is an important lesson for all involved with GLBTQ populations.

By exploring scenarios and stories of everyday people, Marc Adams weaves a cogent argument for creating safe and supportive disclosure reactions. As it shifts the focus to the GLBTQ person coming out, instead of our responses to the phenomenon, it reminds us of who is truly vulnerable.

If you are unsure about this idea or feel that you need more time, this book will prod you to action earlier. Understanding the motivations that drive individuals and families can help us envision a world in which we are all honest.

This insightful volume establishes a case and framework for approaching these critical moments. Read this book with an open mind and open heart. You have the opportunity to support and advocate for someone who needs you, whether a family member, neighbor or friend. Don't miss that chance.

SHELLEY CRAIG, PHD, LCSW

THE GHOST

"I WANTED TO
TELL THE WOMAN
THAT SHE WOULD
NEVER HAVE TO
WORRY ABOUT
DISOWNING HER
SON. I COULD SEE
IN HIS EYES THAT
HE HAD ALREADY
DISOWNED HER. "

I don't believe in ghosts, although I've seen my share of the spooky beings.

Growing up in fundamentalist Christianity, I was taught to believe in demons, not ghosts. The haunting of my own heart, however, had nothing to do with fallen angels.

By the age of 15, I had my own ghost living with me full time.

It was the ghost of the future I was promised was mine.

I was reared by parents who held no shame in teaching their children that living a heterosexual life was the only way to live. That living outside of their idea of "God's plan" was unacceptable.

I bought it. Why wouldn't I? No one taught me that ministers could lie. The future was so planned and perfect the way they described it. Answers were provided for every aspect of my life.

Except I was gay.

I knew it from the age of four. I was sure about my feelings as soon as I laid eyes on Stephen in the first grade.

It didn't bother me that I had those feelings. I certainly did feel somewhat out of place as heterosexuality was the only life promoted at Westmoreland Elementary School.

I saw my first ghost during a church service. The minister had just done a number on homosexuals. After perfectly describing my feelings of being different, he slaughtered me with his declaration that homosexuality was sin. That was the moment I saw the ghost.

It looked a lot like me.

Maybe I should say that it looked a lot like the me for which everyone was hoping.

I'm pretty sure that no one else saw that ghost

that day. I think I did a fairly decent job pretending that I was the same boy they always knew. But inside, I was a much different person. My life would never be the same.

As I got older, I swore I would never tell anyone I was gay. I plotted and schemed how to explain away not having a girlfriend. Those plans fell through when I succumbed to my own idolatry of acceptance and tried to find restorative therapy's place in my life. To begin that process I had to tell someone. Instead of the relief that should come with confession, I felt more fear than I had ever felt in my life.

When I resurfaced after coming to terms with the fact that I didn't need to be restored, I was still too terrorized to think about coming out to anyone. I had a boyfriend and was thousands of miles from my biological family. Most of my friends from high school and university had gone their own way and I expended very little effort to stay in touch with most of them.

Years passed and I realized the significance of coming out. For me to fully live my human experience and possess lasting peace, I must live an honest life.

A part of me wanted to believe no one knew I was gay until I told them. Common sense told me that for the most part it was a confirmation not an announcement.

As the process began, I noticed a striking similarity in disclosure reactions. The moment I chose to be honest about my life somehow became everyone else's moment.

My parents begged for forgiveness for anything they might have done to make me choose to be gay. Other family members required HIV tests and promises I wouldn't molest their children. Friends complained they felt betrayed and walked away.

How did my moment of honesty become their moment of torment?

At the time, I shrugged it off as uneducated people responding as they had been taught. They were believers of the same poorly scripted religious information which seduced me into self-hate.

Six years later, after publishing *The Preacher's Son*, I began speaking at community meetings, universities and other groups. I began to hear the same disclosure reactions I thought were unique to my experience.

As the years rolled on, I noticed that the responses I endured to my coming out were fairly typical. Certainly my biological family had a specific depth to their issues created by their religious lifestyle choice but the root of it was very similar to the experiences of those around me.

"My son just came out to me," one mother said to me. I was speaking at a prominent public university and a student had brought his mother to the lecture.

"Well, that's a great thing," I said. "It means you taught your son to be honest."

"I taught my son to be a man," she said sharply. "I taught my son to show respect to his family."

I looked past the woman's shoulder to see her son furiously blinking back tears. The pain in his eyes was something that I will not forget.

"You don't think I'm a man?" I challenged. She, of course, ignored my question.

"My son is not going to be someone who will ever do anything publicly that will show anyone he is gay."

Anger and impatience crept up from my gut.

"I have already told my son that he will never, never tell anyone else about this. If he ever tells his grandmother he will no longer be my son."

The image of my own grandmother kissing my boyfriend's cheek and leaving a huge smudge of red lipstick on his face burned behind my eyes.

I wanted to tell the woman that she would never

have to worry about disowning her son. I could see in his eyes he had already disowned her. A million words danced on my tongue. Most of them could not be taken back. I swallowed them for the sake of her son.

"I raised my son better than this."

I couldn't look in her eyes. I was afraid I would see yet another sad, scared soul. I was in no frame of mind to feel sympathy for a woman who had just publicly shamed her son, my gay brother.

I took a deep breath and stared at her pursed lips wondering if they had ever kissed anyone out of love.

"I still say you did a great job teaching your son to be honest," I said confidently, knowing the boy was absorbing every word. "Many gay people don't ever get to the point where they are able to be so honest."

The woman left with her son trailing behind. I handed him my HeartStrong card and asked him to email me. I knew that there was very little I could do or say to ease the pain slicing through him. His next steps were in his hands and I felt confident he was courageous enough to move in the right direction.

As we drove on to our next HeartStrong Forum, I could not stop thinking about that mother's insistence on controlling her son's honesty. Her idolatry of acceptance was affecting more than her own life.

Where would a parent get the idea that they could order their son or daughter to lie?

Who gave my parents permission to say that I was going to their Hell because of my self-acceptance?

It was me. It was all of us.

Why We Are Out

"THE BOTTOM LINE
IS THAT GAY OR
STRAIGHT, LIFE IS
TOO SHORT AND
LOVE TOO RARE
NOT TO KISS YOUR
HUSBAND, WIFE,
BOYFRIEND OR
GIRLFRIEND
WHENEVER AND
WHEREVER YOU
FEEL LIKE IT."

It is never too early for someone to begin understanding who they are.

It is never stated that someone is too young to understand that they are heterosexual. During the early years of life, children are encouraged and praised when they interact with other children in a heterosexual manner. Boys and girls are paired at heterosexual weddings, school functions, seating arrangements in classrooms, etc.

I knew I was different at four years old. I realized I was attracted to other boys by third grade, pretty much the same time that heterosexual boys and girls started developing playground crushes on each other.

Rather than scrutinizing children for their search to find where they fit, their growing into their own should be celebrated. Nature has its way of letting us discover ourselves. Stifling it is unnatural.

It does not matter if the person coming out is your child, a friend, co-worker, or a biological family member. If you can comprehend why they are being honest with you, your disclosure reaction will be appropriate.

People must come out due to the myth that everyone is heterosexual, man or woman only, and that you can only be as you appear on the outside.

Throughout time, civilizations have successfully respected or rejected human differences. There are those who have tried to justify their hatred of differences through the narrow vision required by their religion.

Even some people who are perceived as politically and socially liberal find difficulty in respecting GLBT persons, including family members.

Society promotes and rewards heterosexuality. Billboards, bus ads, magazines and much of the internet are decidedly pro-heterosexual. This reinforces the conditioning placed upon children that heterosexuality is the path for everyone.

By coming out to friends, families, co-workers and the world we free ourselves of the bondage such an oppressive climate can create. We are also making the road easier for those who follow us.

Coming out also creates visibility and shows human diversity at its best. It can also show the lack of respect family members have for those coming out. I would be rich if I had a dollar for each time I heard a parent say that it's okay for people to be gay but they are just glad there aren't any gay people in their family. I would be super rich if I had a dollar for every time I heard a parent gloat about how grateful they are that their gay son is not a drag queen or their lesbian daughter is feminine.

Some very misguided parents believe that if they raise their children in a certain way, there is no possibility for their children to be homosexual.

No one chooses orientation or gender identity. The choice is to lie or be honest.

Straight people come out just like gay people. The difference is that society anticipates and rewards those who come out as heterosexual.

Every day is straight pride day. Heterosexuals display their sexuality and orientation in dozens of ways each day. Photos of offspring, in most cases the result of their heterosexuality, are blatantly displayed. Photos and tales of heterosexual husbands, wives, boyfriends and girlfriends are relayed throughout each day.

When a gay or lesbian person attempts the same activities, it can be labeled as flaunting and is discouraged in many environments. The bottom line is that gay or straight, life is too short and love too rare not to kiss your husband, wife, boyfriend or girlfriend whenever and wherever you feel like it.

THE CHOICE

"THE ISSUE IS NOT
WHETHER OR NOT
IT IS A CHOICE.
CAN YOU LOVE
ENOUGH TO SHOW
THEM LOVE
REGARDLESS OF
WHAT THEY TELL
YOU ABOUT
THEMSELVES?"

Some justify respecting their GLBT friends and family because they have decided that it is not a choice.

The issue is not whether or not it is a choice. Can you love enough to show them love regardless of what they tell you about themselves?

Real love is communicated through unconditional expression. When someone comes out to you they are not asking for permission nor are they asking if it is okay for them to accept themselves. It is an announcement.

If someone were able to choose to be gay, lesbian, bisexual or transgender, it wouldn't matter because there is nothing wrong with being gay, lesbian, bisexual or transgender. Overall, the issue of choice always tends to be more about how some justify who and why they will love.

The only choice involved is whether or not you will show unconditional love.

LOVE

"I LOVE YOU NO
MATTER WHAT."

Religion, fear and the idolatry of acceptance often prohibit people from showing love to those coming out.

In my book, *(lost)*Found, I wrote that I believe that forgiveness is a gift. If you have been negative or selfish in your response to someone coming out to you, it can be difficult to undo though not impossible. Most of us coming out assume that we will face rejection or a reprimand from someone who doesn't understand.

Apologizing for a negative disclosure reaction is an excellent start. Nothing heals a wrong like an apology from the heart. The humility it takes to admit you were selfish can turn the situation around. If you are not confident to seek good information on your own, ask the person who came out to you.

There is nothing wrong with apologizing, asking for information and seeking time to educate yourself. Asking that same person to help you find accurate information is the next step in moving beyond a poor disclosure reaction on your part.

For any relationship grounded in love, acknowledged mistakes can become part of the past. In knowing that forgiveness is gift, remember that you need to ask for it.

Love is key in your disclosure reaction. There are those who say that people who are coming out are the same person they always were. They are different in that they are finally honest. Being an honest person changes everything.

Unconditional love exists in the hearts of people regardless of religious affiliation. Unless requested, there is no need for a religious response, positive or negative.

True love is unconditional. Verbal reassurance of your love is the best first step and reaction.

THE GIFT

"COMING OUT
IS A GIFT OF
HONESTY."

For some, the drama kicks into high gear when someone comes out to them. Some simply stop listening to what is being said and immediately look inward for a quick fix to revise the news.

With parents it usually starts with choosing to blame themselves for what they assume is a problem. Many parents mistake the honesty of coming out as a cry for help.

"We want to apologize for anything we've done in the past to make this happen."

Those were some of the first words my parents said to me after I came out to them. My first thought was how ridiculous it was that they assumed they were responsible for my sexual orientation. My second thought was that I was right in my assumption that they knew absolutely nothing about homosexuality. But I had empathy. What they knew about homosexuality was what they learned in church from heterosexuals. In general, it's always best to talk to an out gay person to find out what it means and what it's like to be gay.

There is no need to create drama and blame yourself when someone comes out. Like the person coming out, parents have no control or influence over gender identity, expression or sexual orientation. As much power as a parent may feel they have in their children's lives, this is an area in which they have absolutely no influence.

Coming out is a gift of honesty. It is the act of giving this gift that is best responded to, not the content of the message.

Insincerity is easily detected. Your response should not be anything but honest.

If you are experiencing negative feelings, talk about them to the person being honest with you. Just usually not at the moment they are coming out to you. Remember, this moment is not about you. It's about the person coming out.

If your disclosure reaction is negative or even selfish, look into your heart to find out why someone else's honesty makes you feel uncomfortable.

Some people identify stages everyone goes through as they process a GLBT person's honesty with them. While that may be true for some, it doesn't have to be true for everyone.

You may feel fear, shame, shock or combinations of the three. Challenge yourself. What is the person feeling who is being honest with you? This the moment to think about their feelings. If you are feeling fear, shame or shock, think about what that person has had to go through to get to this place. Most people come out after deep personal introspection and turbulent self-denial.

Remember, they are not telling you that you are gay, lesbian, bisexual or transgender. It's about them and their quest for an honest life.

Coming out is a gift of honesty.

Many of my friends were forced out after their parents ransacked their bedrooms and found revealing literature or pornography. Ironically, this is also how some of my friend's parents were able to confirm their assumption that their offspring were heterosexual.

Others were forced out when their parents hacked into their computers, reading emails and other information. Still others are outed by schools (religious, private and public), or religious leadership.

What motivates someone to come out is not so important. It is the act of coming out that is reason to celebrate.

Even in the midst of a forced outing, the task of announcing sexual orientation or gender identity takes an incredible amount of courage. It's courage that heterosexuals sometimes find difficult to comprehend.

If you are a family member, you are among the people agonized over the most. Regardless of how close your family may be, most GLBT people are still unsure about telling their families.

When a family member comes out, they are giving you a gift. You can choose to accept the gift with happiness. You may also choose to reject it. Chances are that if you reject the gift, you will not be receiving gifts in the future. If you choose to reject the gift, you can be sure that it will be re-gifted. And you can be sure that the recipient of the re-gift will be receiving all future gifts.

Gift cards are not available. You are not able to take this gift and make it into what you want.

Journey to Myself

Alexander Pangborn

"MY PARENTS ACKNOWLEDGE THAT AT TIMES IT SEEMED TO BE MORE ABOUT THEM AND THEIR ADJUSTMENT THAN MY DISCOVERING HOW TO BE A GAY/TRANS-IDENTIFIED PERSON."

Coming out is never an easy process.

It takes skill to maintain focus on your personal journey and to balance your needs with the needs of those closest to you. Coming out twice is even trickier.

I came out to the world as a lesbian when I was 16. I had known for two years that I identified as gay and when the time finally came to tell others, I made sure that everyone knew. My parents were not the first to be told, but their reaction meant the most to me.

When I finally felt able to reveal myself to my parents, it was a relief. The worst case scenario I played out time and time again in my mind was not meant for my life story. But it was by no means a cake walk. My parents were shocked by the revelation. Although they tried their best to remain stoic, I know they hoped I was wrong, it was a phase and life would eventually return to their idea of normal.

I bullied them into attending a PFLAG (Parents, Families and Friends of Gays) meeting claiming I needed to meet more gay people and find a stronger support network. So they took me to meetings, politely listening to other parents share their stories. My parents soon shared their story of having a gay child and, eventually, became the co-chairs of the local PFLAG chapter.

Almost six years later, feeling fully accepted as a lesbian and supported by my family, I came out again as transgender. This seemed like a much bigger bombshell than revealing that I was gay. Everyone seemed convinced that whatever I was seeking, I was looking for answers in all the wrong places.

My parents, believing that I was confused and unsure of whether or not to take the next step, offered to pay for my chest surgery. They have since told me that this was an attempt to call my bluff and that they expected me to back down and put off transitioning. Imagine their shock when I readily accepted and called the surgeon to schedule my surgery date!

Four months later, my partner, parents and I flew to San Francisco for my chest surgery. Everyone was still convinced that this could be a big mistake, but stoically stood by my side and provided what support they could. It wasn't until after my surgery that I felt a shift in my parent's perception.

I will never forget the first day I saw the results of my surgery. On the first day I was allowed to shower after the procedure, I undressed in front of the bathroom mirror. When I saw my reflection in the mirror, I began to cry. My partner, worried that I had hurt myself, rushed to see if I was alright.

"This is the first time I've ever looked in the mirror and seen what I thought I should," I said.

That moment created a great shift, allowing my family to clearly see that the path was the right one for me. Instead of regret, I was able to show relief and happiness and that, in turn, helped erase my parent's fear and doubt.

In retrospect, my parents acknowledge that I assumed the caretaker role when I came out to them. When speaking about their journey, my parents have said that I took their hands and lead them through the process of learning about and accepting having a gay/trans child. My parents acknowledge that at times it seemed to be more about them and their adjustment than my discovering how to be a gay/trans-identified person walking in this world.

I understand this and I do not hold it against them. Those who are closest to us are also going through a transition. They are learning to see and accept us for who we are and letting go of the expectations which don't always match our hopes and dreams.

I have seen countless parents turn a coming out

into their own personal tragedy-recounting the story over and over for years for a captive audience without ever really listening to themselves or learning from what they are saying. Somewhere in the process, their own identity is lost. They begin to identify only as parents of a gay/trans person.

It's easy to focus on your own shock, disappointment or anger. Eventually, those things need to be released if you hope to keep your loved one in your life. At some point there needs to be a return to your own identity as a person who has a gay/trans child.

I am one of the lucky ones. I had parents who stood by me, regardless of their initial misgivings. They poured their hearts and souls into making sure that I could walk in this world the way I needed to, and making sure I knew I was loved and respected. Once they felt this was clear they again became just my parents. My parents who love to travel, and garden, and spend time with their family, and who happen to have a transgender son.

ALEXANDER PANGBORN

HUMAN
KINDNESS

"IT IS POSSIBLE TO PUT ASIDE WHAT OTHERS HAVE TAUGHT YOU AND SIMPLY LOOK AT THE FACE OF THE PERSON COMING OUT TO YOU. SEE THE PERSON IN FRONT OF YOU AS THEY ARE."

Sexual orientation and gender identity are not a religious issue.

We have permitted an unholy union between homosexuality and religion. We never admonish the media when they present the subject for discussion. There is always a gay person (religious or not) and the opposing person is always a person identifying by a particular religious belief. This allowance has permeated our society and perpetrated the fallacy that being GLBT has something to do with religion.

GLBT people come from every religious and non-religious upbringing. Their families are Atheist, Jewish, Mormon, Scientologist, Baptist, Wiccan and every other ideology. Subscribing to religion does not weaken or strengthen the possibility of someone being gay, lesbian, bisexual or transgender.

If your religion teaches you that you should hate the sin but love the sinner, you will need to make a decision.

Religious beliefs are one of the main reasons why GLBT people are forced to sacrifice relationships with friends and family.

What is often unwelcome and unhealthy to GLBT people is when those they come out to (and others) use religious beliefs to disparage their act of honesty and their life.

It doesn't really matter what the Bible or any other book has to say about homosexuality. Either you love your children, friends or family members or you don't. Your definition of love is not applicable in this situation. What is applicable is the definition of love possessed by the person being honest with you.

For some, the choice of religion over family is not up for discussion which usually results in loss of human relationships or at the least, extremely strained interactions.

There are dozens of books dissecting religion based anti-GLBT opinions and attempts to reconcile that particular religion with sexual orientation and gender identity. There are dozens more published to convince you that you are right in withholding respect for those same people.

If your religious beliefs require you to distrust your heart, it is very difficult to follow your heart instead of listening to other people tell you what to do. In the long run it's best to follow your heart instead of learned head knowledge acquired by listening to people who aren't GLBT or who have chosen to discard their GLBT heritage to live a simulated heterosexual lifestyle.

It is possible to put aside what others have taught you and simply look at the face of the person coming out to you. What helps the most at that moment is to see the person as they are.

That person is not a religious text, an anecdote in a sermon, a sinner, or a saint. They are your child, your parent, your spiritual advisor, your co-worker, your closest friend, your sister, your brother, your mother or your father. Simply put, they are a human being.

You may never know the endless nights of soul-searching and the years of slow burning denial that were overcome to bring them to your door with the gift of honesty.

If they share your religious background, you can be sure that they have already anticipated any religious advice you feel obligated to give. Every religious text and every possible out are considered and tested for validity. The strength of the human spirit has brought them to this moment of self acceptance. The power of human kindness will give them a world of peace.

THE
THREE C'S

We must be
courageous.

We must be
confident.

We must be
consistent.

Often the right thing to do is the hardest thing to do. Coming out is most likely one of the hardest and yet one of the most important things a person can do.

It takes courage to do the right thing, especially when society reinforces the lie that the heterosexual lifestyle is somehow proper for every human being. Nothing on this journey defeats a life lived honestly.

An honest life is a life lived courageously. The pressure to live a dishonest life comes at us from every direction. Living life with courage allows us to close our eyes each night and sleep in peace. Leaving behind the idolatry of acceptance sets everyone free to find the place in their heart where courage waits to be unchained.

Confidence is not easy. More often than not doubt prevails and we close the door to living with confidence. When our social surroundings encourage dependency on acceptance from others instead of self-acceptance, achieving self-confidence seems a pointless endeavor.

To live life with confidence we must first look to our own heart. The same heart we looked to in the middle of our darkest moments before coming out. Think you were the only person to feel the intense loneliness associated with self-denial? Think again. It felt like you were alone those nights when you used to wish for death rather than wake to another day. But you were never really alone. All around others traveled the same road.

That same introspection must be revisited in order to find that mark where you can begin to live a confident life.

Each day lived with confidence leads to a life lived confidently. Days become weeks and months and without notice, confidence in yourself and who you are becomes a natural part of your existence and expression.

Finding a path to living with courage, taking that courage and living with confidence paves the way to living our lives consistently.

Those who don't understand the importance of us living life honestly should be exposed to our lives lived consistently. Hesitation on our part could cause family or friends to doubt our honesty.

Not only does living life consistently show others the courage to be ourselves, it also strengthens our resolve to live confidently.

IT'S
NOT ABOUT
YOU

understanding coming out & self-acceptance

[signature: Marc Adams]

MARC ADAMS

FOREWORD BY SHELLEY CRAIG, PhD, LCSW
CONTRIBUTING AUTHOR ALEXANDER PANGBORN

WWW.WINDOWBOOKSONLINE.COM